Another book written by Madden
Tanner and Tovah Tanner

**Royale Boy Blue
Struggles with His Etiquette**

Royale Boy Blue Becomes A Master Builder

By: Madden Tanner and Tovah Tanner

Illustrations by: Claude Harris III

Madeleen E. Tanner

ISBN-13: 978-1548746322
ISBN-10: 1548746320

DEDICATION

I am a proud Jr. FLL member of aSTEAM Village, a
Robotics team in Kansas City, Missouri, and a member of the
National Society of Black Engineers
also known as, NSBE.

This book is dedicated to all the supporters who donated
towards my Robotics Competition Fundraiser Campaign that
was hosted in 2016. I reached my goal of $2,000 and was able
to attend the 42nd Annual National Society of Black
Engineers Competition in Boston, Massachusetts.
Thank you all for the support!

Love ~ Madden

Hi! My name is, Madden Tanner, also known as Royale Boy Blue. I love to read, draw, build cool creations, and study STEM. Do you want to be a Master Builder someday? If so, follow your dream because you can become anything you want to be. **Imagine It, Draw It, Build It!**

Royale Boy Blue was only two years old when he got his first set of foam building blocks. They were soft, brightly colored, and great for developing creativity. Royale Boy Blue would stack block after block while imagining he was a king in a big, colorful castle, ruler of the Land

of Happiness. Royale's imagination was unique and it showed through his creations. His father, Mr. Blue, would always tell him, "Practice makes perfect." So, for fun, Royale would build a design and quickly tear it down to create something bigger and better.

By the age of four, Royale had graduated from foam blocks and moved on to oversized blocks with interlocking connecting points. He would imagine being a time traveler, racing back through time to explore historic places all over the world. He would travel there by train,

airplane or automobile, all of which he built himself. By the age of six, Royale began to draw the designs that he imagined, in the hopes of becoming a Master Builder. He had no idea that soon, his imagination, and love of building would take him places he never imagined.

It was a summer day when Royale's mother, Mrs. Blue, decided to research STEM programs. STEM is an acronym that stands for Science, Technology, Engineering, and Mathematics. Though she searched and searched, she couldn't find many teams in

their area. Undeterred, she began taking Royale to building competitions around the city. Every time Royale participated in a competition, his excitement increased. After each outing, he would rush home and pull out all his bricks to practice new designs.

Several months passed before Mrs. Blue finally received an email from a local STEM team. The email read: Thank you for registering Royale Boy Blue for aSTEAM Village 9th Community STEM Day and Conference. Your registration number is 12292008. Our STEM team also

includes art, architecture, and agriculture. We look forward to seeing you at the event on October 7, 2015 from 12 PM to 4 PM. "Oh, Royale," she called out, "I have great news!" Royale came running toward the living room, eager to see what had his mother so excited.

"Yes, ma'am," he said as he came bounding around the corner. "A local STEM team has accepted your registration! They are hosting a STEM conference on Sunday. Would you like to go?" she asked. "Yay, I sure do, Mom!" Royale said happily. In a flash, he ran to the

den to tell his father the amazing news. The French doors went flying open with a loud BOOM. "Dad, Dad, Dad, guess what?" he shouted. "What is it, Son?" said his father. "I've been accepted to attend a STEM conference nearby. "Well, Congratulations!"

his father said with a big smile on his face. All week, Royale crossed out the days on his calendar until finally he had only one day left. That night, he could barely sleep. He tossed and turned, dreaming about what STEM day would be like.

"Good morning, Little Rose Bud. Today is STEM Day," Mrs. Blue said early the next morning. Royale quickly jumped out of bed. "Good morning, Mom," he blurted out. In a hurry, he showered, and put on his clothes. He dressed in blue slacks and a white button-down

shirt with his signature, one-of-a-kind bow tie. Royale loves wearing bow ties! "Good morning, Bluuue," his brother, Jamari, said in his special way, dragging out his brother's name like he always did. "You seem to be in a hurry. Where are you going?" "Mom is taking me to a day full

of STEM. I apologize, but I'm going to miss your boxing match today," Royale said. "It's okay, Little Brother. Dad will be with me. Have fun! I'll hear all about it at dinner. See you later, Bluuue," said Jamari. After Royale ate his breakfast, he grabbed his backpack and filled it

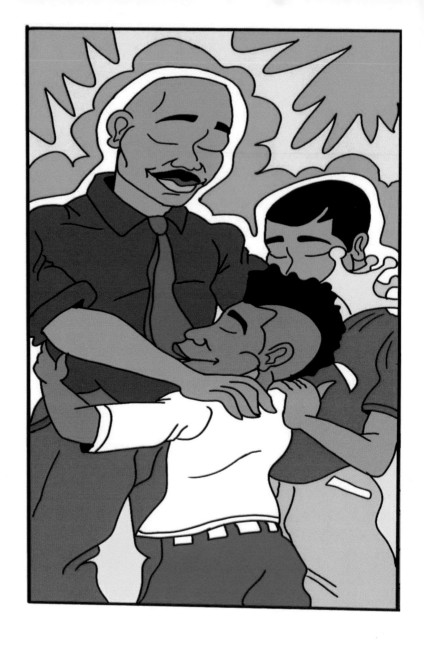

with a few of his science detective books, healthy snacks, and a bottle of water. "I love you," Royale said as he gave his dad and brother a hug. It was a short drive to the conference. "We have arrived at the location," Royale announced excitedly as they pulled into

the parking lot. "There goes Kaden," said Royale, pointing at his friend by the entrance. He rushed closer to the building to get his attention. "You're here? Oh Royale, isn't this cool?" said Kaden, happily surprised to see a friend. "Let's go inside," said Mrs. Blue.

Once inside, he was amazed to see so many people. The room was filled with parents, conference organizers and other children. Each room had a different STEM theme. They had computer coding, building brick stations and a water filtration station that showed everyone

how to clean water. Excited by what he learned, Royale signed a contract and became an official member of the aSTEAM Village Robotics team. As a new member, he promised to honor the STEM core values: work as a team, show respect, and share your discoveries.

Royale and his mother arrived home just in time for dinner. They were greeted with the awesome smell of freshly cooked veggie burgers. "Congratulations!" his father and brother shouted as they stood beside the dining table wearing white chef jackets and hats.

On the table were homemade veggie brick burgers loaded with lettuce, ketchup, and pickles, complete with homemade potato chips, dipping sauce and a tall glass of fresh lemonade. Royale was so surprised. He couldn't believe his dad did all this just for him.

"Wash your hands and come tell me all about your day," Mr. Blue said. Royale did just that and filled his dad in on all the cool things he learned and interesting people he met. He also mentioned that Coach Wells spoke with all the members about earning a chance to enter in

the nationwide robotics competition in Boston, Massachusetts. "It would be just like I imagined. In three months, I will travel to Boston by way of a super-fast train, airplane or maybe an automobile," said Royale excitedly. Later, that night, his mother, and father

discussed ways to raise money so Royale could travel to Boston with his Robotics team. "I talked to one of the parents about creating a campaign to help raise funds for his travel expenses," said Mrs. Blue. "Do you think we can raise the funds in such a short amount of

time?" Mr. Blue asked. "It doesn't hurt to try," said Mrs. Blue optimistically. The next day, she created a fundraiser campaign called Royale Boy Blue's Robotics Championship Fund – Trip to Boston. Within two months, Royale's campaign had reached his goal of $2,000!

Their friends, family and inspired members of the community came together and were able to send him to the competition. After months of hard work, it was finally time to showcase their solar-powered robot in Boston. This futuristic robot filtered pollutants from the air, helping

to create a healthier environment for people, plants, and food crops. The day of the flight had arrived. At the terminal, Royale noticed that the wings of the plane extended in two dimensions. It was all white with a red tip, just like he had imagined. For the next four hours,

the team enjoyed free Wi-Fi and awesome aerial views. After the plane landed, everyone rounded up their luggage and took a bus straight to the convention center. It was colossal! It had a siphonic roof draining system, V-shaped pillars, and countless glass

windows. "Our effective teamwork got us here. Let's go in and be efficient with our STEM presentation," said Coach Wells. The team presented the solar-powered robot as the other competitors and judges gazed at their creation in amazement. Shortly after the scores were

tallied, it was time to announce the winners. Royale and his teammates sat nervously in the crowd. Then, the presenter came to the stage to announce the winners. "The first-place STEM award for the 42nd Annual Robotics Competition goes to aSTEAM Village!"

The crowd cheered loudly while the team walked to the stage. Every member on the team received a shiny gold medal that read, STEM. Just like that, Royale Boy Blue became a

Master Builder!

IMAGINE IT, DRAW IT, BUILD IT

DRAW A FUTURISTIC ROBOT

ABOUT AUTHOR

Madden Tanner, is a smart and ambitious 3rd grader, that is soaring through his homeschool studies. His curriculum also includes African culture, STEM, dance, acting, agriculture and entrepreneurship. In 2014, with the assistance

of his parents, Madden created and facilitates R.O.Y.A.L.E Boy Book Club. R.O.Y.A.L.E is an acronym that stands for Reach Outgoing Youth Accelerate Literacy Enthusiasm. Membership is offered to boys ages 5-12 years old in the Kansas City, Missouri surrounding community.

Made in the USA
Columbia, SC
18 March 2018